TIMELINES FROM INDIAN HISTORY

TIMELINES FROM INDIAN HISTORY

From ancient civilizations to a modern democracy

Editors Ayushi Thapliyal, Vatsal Verma
US Editor Jennette ElNaggar
Project Art Editors Devika Awasthi, Bhavika Mathur
Art Editor and Illustrator Priyal Mote
Jacket Designers Bhavika Mathur, Priyal Mote, Priyanka Thakur
Senior Picture Researcher Sumedha Chopra
DTP Designers Narender Kumar, Rajdeep Singh
Senior DTP Designer Tarun Sharma
Pre-Production Manager Sunil Sharma
Production Manager Pankaj Sharma
Picture Research Manager Taiyaba Khatoon
Managing Editor Chitra Subramanyam
Managing Art Editor Neha Ahuja Chowdhry
Senior Managing Art Editor Priyanka Thakur
Managing Director, India Aparna Sharma

Author Anurima Chanda
Research and additional text by Megh Mazumdar, Kudrat Singh

First American Edition, 2021
Published in the United States by DK Publishing
1450 Broadway, Suite 801, New York, NY 10018

A catalog record for this book is available
from the Library of Congress.
ISBN 978-0-7440-5454-5

Printed and bound in India

For the curious
www.dk.com

This book was made with Forest Stewardship Council ™
certified paper – one small step in DK's commitment
to a sustainable future.
For more information go to www.dk.com/our-green-pledge

About the book

Timelines from Indian History attempts to tell an inclusive story of India from the prehistoric to contemporary times. The women and men who have conceptualized, written, edited, and designed the book have tried to reflect the diversity of India and the lives and cultures of its people. While this is not a comprehensive history of India, given its incredible breadth and diversity, the team has attempted to include more than just the country's milestones. They have also tried to showcase the voices of those communities that have traditionally been overshadowed or excluded from mainstream history.

Traveling through time

The earliest events in this book took place a very long time ago. Some dates may be followed by "million years ago" or "years ago." Other dates have BCE and CE after them. These are short for "before the Common Era" and "Common Era." The Common Era dates from when people think Jesus was born. Where the exact date of an event is not known, "c." is used. This is short for the Latin word circa, meaning "around," and indicates that the date is approximate.

Names of territories

This book uses the contemporary names of countries and cities. Names such as India, Pakistan, and Afghanistan have been used to indicate the region in the modern context, in pages that precede contemporary timelines.

CONTENTS

5 INDIA AFTER INDEPENDENCE

1947–2020

1
PREHISTORY AND THE BEGINNINGS

4,600 million years ago-200 BCE

Formation of India

Millions of years ago, India was not part of Asia at all. The landmass drifted across prehistoric oceans to join the Asian mainland. As it adapted to the local climate, the flora and fauna underwent changes. The region became populated with early humans who migrated from Africa, and, over time, civilizations emerged. Written records are absent for this period of prehistory, so most of our knowledge is archaeological—from the study of tools, bones, and objects left behind.

200 million years ago
Gondwana, previously a part of Pangea, splits and forms South America, Africa, Australia, Antarctica, and India.

80 million years ago
India separates from Madagascar and drifts northward toward Asia.

50 to 40 million years ago
The subcontinent of India covers 5,590 miles (9,000 km) in 70 million years—fast for a plate—and rams into Asia, giving rise to the Himalayas.

2 million years ago
Early Indian ancestors begin using stone tools.

300 million years ago
All continents that we know of today are part of one big supercontinent—Pangea.

180 million years ago
India, Antarctica, and Madagascar are a part of the same plate as Africa, until they rift apart.

65 million years ago
The Indian plate crosses a number of hot spots on its journey northward, turns lighter, and picks up speed.

1.8 million years ago
A large section of modern humans migrate from Africa and settle in the subcontinent.

130,000 years ago
Tools become more refined, smaller and thinner, and flake blades emerge.

Breakup of Pangea

Shifts in the mantle layer below the Earth's surface cause Pangea to break into Laurasia in the north (consisting much of North America, Europe, and Asia) and Gondwana in the south, separated by the Tethys Sea.

Hot spots

Hot spots are extremely hot regions under the Earth's surface. While passing over one such spot—the Reunion hot spot—volcanic action causes basaltic lava to pour from the peninsular Indian region forming the Deccan Plateau.

The Himalayas

The Indian plate continues to push into the Eurasian plate. As a result, even today, the Himalayas continue to grow at a speed of 0.4 in (1 cm) per year.

Early humans

Homo habilis and *Homo erectus*, the ancestors of humans, create sharp pebble-flake tools by striking one stone against another. They possibly also use a series of sounds to communicate, quite similar to how we use words today.

75,000 years ago
Modern humans first appear in India.

6000 BCE
Humans domesticate animals and hunt wild ones.

4000 BCE
The potter's wheel is imported from West Asia and pottery flourishes.

2600 BCE
The first great cities such as Mohenjo-Daro and Harappa emerge as part of the Indus Valley Civilization.

300 BCE
The Brahmi script develops. Most other modern Indian scripts originate from it.

34,000–24,000 years ago
Initially cave dwellers, human groups now settle down in primitive huts.

7000–5000 BCE
Houses become multiroomed and farming begins.

3000 BCE
Cultivation of rice, mainly in the Gangetic River valley, begins.

1000 BCE ...
Advancements are made in iron technology, and people replace stone weapons with metal ones.

Early human lifestyle

Early humans live in caves. As they start farming, settlements come up. Houses are built of sun-dried mud bricks of regular sizes. People weave baskets and cloth. The dead are buried with ornaments. A clear distinction between the rich and the poor is also seen during this time.

Metallurgy

With the discovery of copper and bronze, humans find an alternative to stone tools. But the quantity of metal extraction is less in the early period and it takes some time for it to fully replace stone.

Early cities

Technological advances result in villages expanding into towns and then cities. Trade flourishes and humans start living in an organized manner.

Writing

Writing scripts develop, moving from pictographic versions to the modern ones. People start documenting their lives in the written format. The period of prehistory comes to an end.

Bronze and Iron Ages

As farming settlements northwest of the Indian subcontinent developed into sprawling urban centers, India's first Bronze Age civilization was born. Several other copper-using or Chalcolithic cultures developed at the same time with distinctive pottery styles. In the next millennia, technological developments brought about the Iron Age. These developments impacted early Indians and their livelihoods.

> " ... the Bronze Age cities were dominated by the religio-political structure of power and subsisted on the food surplus drawn from the hinterland. The Cities of Iron Age were mostly commercial centers with a non-ecclesiastical political system."
>
> *VK Thakur in the journal Indian History Congress, 1979*

Decline of Indus Valley Civilization

City life begins to deteriorate in the Indus Valley. The quality of pottery, beads, and seals drops and population reduces. Long-distance trade breaks down. Flimsy houses replace the grand architecture of the earlier urban centers. This transition could be because of flood or drought, the breakdown of trade with West and Central Asia, invasions, or the fall of a unifying state.

c.1900 BCE

Vedas and the Indo-Aryans

The Indo-Aryans, a community from Central Asia, arrive in India from the northwest. The *Rig Veda* is composed in c.1500 BCE. This collection of hymns is transferred orally before being written down centuries later. The Vedas include sacrificial rituals. The economy is largely pastoral and based on agriculture. Occupations, such as barbers, carpenters, weavers, and craftspeople also exist as per Vedic literature. Slavery is practiced and many of the enslaved are prisoners of war.

c. 2000–1500 BCE

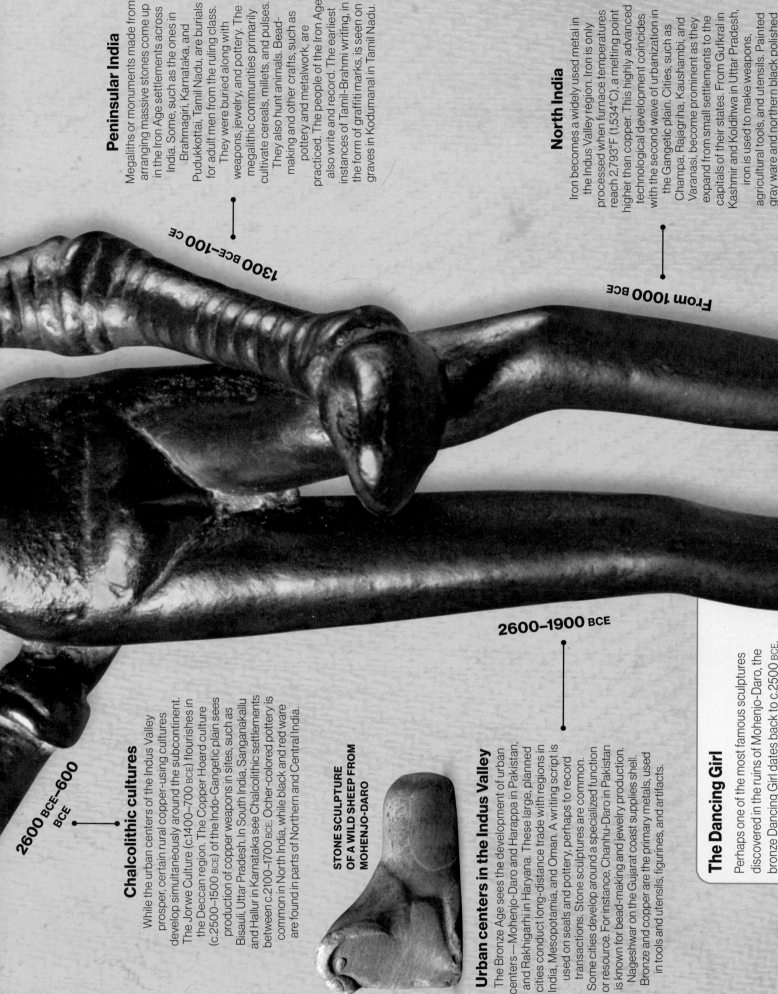

Peninsular India

Megaliths or monuments made from arranging massive stones come up in the Iron Age settlements across India. Some, such as the ones in Brahmagiri, Karnataka, and Pudukkottai, Tamil Nadu, are burials for adult men from the ruling class. They were buried along with weapons, jewelry, and pottery. The megalithic communities primarily cultivate cereals, millets, and pulses. They also hunt animals. Bead-making and other crafts, such as pottery and metalwork, are practiced. The people of the Iron Age also write and record. The earliest instances of Tamil-Brahmi writing, in the form of graffiti marks, is seen on graves in Kodumanal in Tamil Nadu.

1300 BCE–100 CE

North India

Iron becomes a widely used metal in the Indus Valley region. Iron is only processed when furnace temperatures reach 2,793°F (1,534°C), a melting point higher than copper. This highly advanced technological development coincides with the second wave of urbanization in the Gangetic plain. Cities, such as Champa, Rajagriha, Kaushambi, and Varanasi, become prominent as they expand from small settlements to the capitals of their states. From Gufkral in Kashmir and Koldihwa in Uttar Pradesh, iron is used to make weapons, agricultural tools, and utensils. Painted gray ware and northern black polished ware are the defining pottery styles.

From 1000 BCE

2600–1900 BCE

2600 BCE–600 BCE

Chalcolithic cultures

While the urban centers of the Indus Valley prosper, certain rural copper-using cultures develop simultaneously around the subcontinent. The Jorwe Culture (c.1400–700 BCE) flourishes in the Deccan region. The Copper Hoard culture (c.2500–1500 BCE) of the Indo-Gangetic plain sees production of copper weapons in sites, such as Bisauli, Uttar Pradesh. In South India, Sanganakallu and Hallur in Karnataka see Chalcolithic settlements between c.2100–1700 BCE. Ocher-colored pottery is common in North India, while black and red ware are found in parts of Northern and Central India.

STONE SCULPTURE OF A WILD SHEEP FROM MOHENJO-DARO

Urban centers in the Indus Valley

The Bronze Age sees the development of urban centers—Mohenjo-Daro and Harappa in Pakistan, and Rakhigarhi in Haryana. These large, planned cities conduct long-distance trade with regions in India, Mesopotamia, and Oman. A writing script is used on seals and pottery, perhaps to record transactions. Stone sculptures are common. Some cities develop around a specialized function or resource. For instance, Chanhu-Daro in Pakistan is known for bead-making and jewelry production. Nageshwar on the Gujarat coast supplies shell. Bronze and copper are the primary metals, used in tools and utensils, figurines, and artifacts.

The Dancing Girl

Perhaps one of the most famous sculptures discovered in the ruins of Mohenjo-Daro, the bronze Dancing Girl dates back to c.2500 BCE. The statue is of a standing young woman, one hand on her waist, wearing bangles and perhaps a necklace. The artist employed the "lost wax" method to make the statue, using a mold covered in clay coating to create the wax model.

Towns and Cities

Much before the modern cities of skyscrapers and planned living spaces, there were basic structures whose sole purpose was to provide shelter and safety to communities. Over time, these grew into villages and towns. As trade opportunities emerged and populations increased, newer forms of administrative control developed. Technology led to job creation and the evolution of towns into metropolises and smart cities.

Community living
Humans live in the open, caves, and rock shelters. They settle closer to rivers and domesticate animals. These hunter-gatherers forage in groups. Tools are made out of stones, animal bones, and wood. They use fire to cook meat.

The first port town
Lothal, a city from Indus Valley Civilization, in Gujarat, emerges as a port town. It has thick walls of almost 65 ft (20 m) to protect residents from floods and high tides.

Rise of the mahanagaras
Sixteen *Mahajanapadas* (republic oligarchies) emerge. Within these are *mahanagaras*, or big cities, with walls, gates, watchtowers, and a bustling urban life.

Small towns
The subcontinent is dotted with small towns and landowners who build large fortified homes around these. The towns have market places for produce. Landowners levy taxes on artisans and traders. Versions of these towns continue to exist today.

150,000–10,000 years ago

7,000 years ago

c.3700 BCE

c.3300–1300 BCE

c.600 BCE

c.6th century CE

c.8th century CE

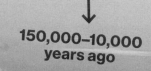

Farming settlements
Communities in Mehrgarh, Pakistan, build mud brick houses with roofs and cubicles for food storage. There is a dramatic change in tools with sharper axes, digging blades, and mullers. Historians call this the Neolithic Revolution, highlighting a shift toward agricultural settlements.

Planned towns
Nomadic communities settle as seen in the Indus Valley town of Mohenjo-Daro. Large platforms above flood level with walls indicate township planning. There is also evidence of spaces for streets and elaborate drainage systems.

Administrative centers
Thanjavur, the capital of the Chola Dynasty in Tamil Nadu, emerges as an important administrative center and temple town. The kings commission architects to build temples that attract pilgrims who give big donations.

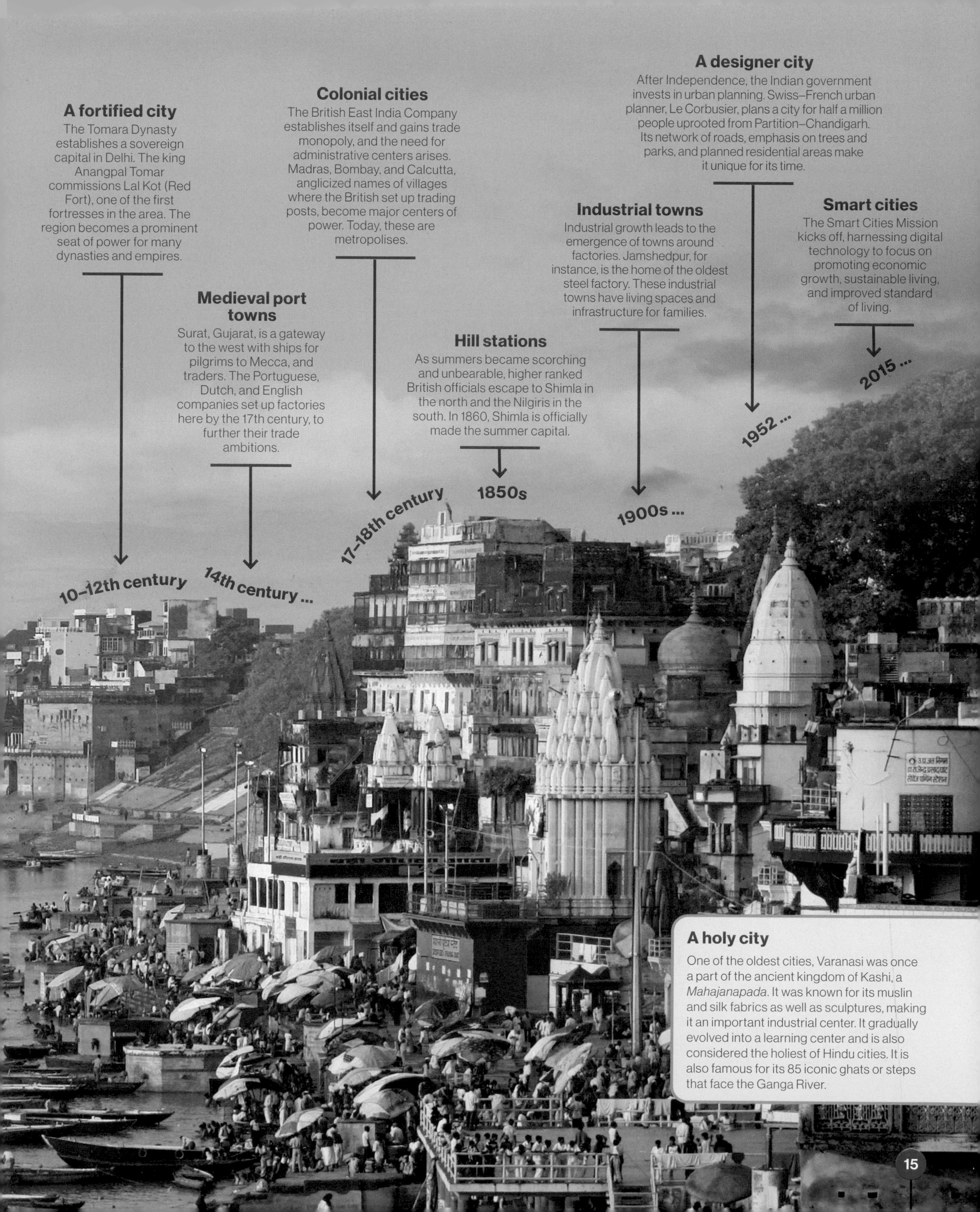

A fortified city
The Tomara Dynasty establishes a sovereign capital in Delhi. The king Anangpal Tomar commissions Lal Kot (Red Fort), one of the first fortresses in the area. The region becomes a prominent seat of power for many dynasties and empires.

10–12th century

Medieval port towns
Surat, Gujarat, is a gateway to the west with ships for pilgrims to Mecca, and traders. The Portuguese, Dutch, and English companies set up factories here by the 17th century, to further their trade ambitions.

14th century ...

Colonial cities
The British East India Company establishes itself and gains trade monopoly, and the need for administrative centers arises. Madras, Bombay, and Calcutta, anglicized names of villages where the British set up trading posts, become major centers of power. Today, these are metropolises.

17–18th century

Hill stations
As summers became scorching and unbearable, higher ranked British officials escape to Shimla in the north and the Nilgiris in the south. In 1860, Shimla is officially made the summer capital.

1850s

Industrial towns
Industrial growth leads to the emergence of towns around factories. Jamshedpur, for instance, is the home of the oldest steel factory. These industrial towns have living spaces and infrastructure for families.

1900s ...

A designer city
After Independence, the Indian government invests in urban planning. Swiss–French urban planner, Le Corbusier, plans a city for half a million people uprooted from Partition–Chandigarh. Its network of roads, emphasis on trees and parks, and planned residential areas make it unique for its time.

1952 ...

Smart cities
The Smart Cities Mission kicks off, harnessing digital technology to focus on promoting economic growth, sustainable living, and improved standard of living.

2015 ...

A holy city
One of the oldest cities, Varanasi was once a part of the ancient kingdom of Kashi, a *Mahajanapada*. It was known for its muslin and silk fabrics as well as sculptures, making it an important industrial center. It gradually evolved into a learning center and is also considered the holiest of Hindu cities. It is also famous for its 85 iconic ghats or steps that face the Ganga River.

Bhimbetka Rock Shelters

Located in the foothills of the Vindhya range in Central India's Madhya Pradesh, the rock shelters or caves of Bhimbetka were once home to early humans. The interiors (right), covered in linear paintings of white and red ocher, represent prehistoric art, possibly India's oldest human art. They depict what life was like for early Indians. Some show humans on horses or with weapons, while others are of animals, such as elephants and horses, or battle scenes. Many paintings are superimposed on older ones and suggest the evolution of art through prehistoric times.

THE ARAB CONQUEST OF SINDH

A new power arrives

There were several instances of failed invasions, all in an attempt to gain a foothold in the Indian subcontinent that also included the present country of Afghanistan. Then came the Arab army of Muhammad bin Qasim who conquered the region of Sindh in 712 CE. This victory would mold and change India's political and cultural landscape for centuries to come.

A ship is plundered

Small kingdoms dot the Indian subcontinent. Trade between Arabia and parts of India and Ceylon flourishes. However, historians believe that the relationship sours after a ship full of gifts from the ruler of Ceylon to Arabia is attacked by pirates near Sindh. The news reaches the powerful governor of Iraq, Al-Hajjaj, in **710**. He asks the ruler of Sindh, Raja Dahir, for justice but receives no favorable reply. This enrages him. He persuades the head of the Umayyad Caliphate, Caliph Walid, to give him permission to attack Sindh, in Pakistan.

The conquest begins

Two attacks in **711** yield no result, as the armies are killed or return defeated. Al-Hajjaj then sends his young nephew Muhammad bin Qasim, a very capable military commander, to lead the campaign against Dahir. A huge army with five catapults is assembled and Debal, an ancient port city in Pakistan on the Indus River, is ransacked. Qasim's army lays siege to the city for the next three days as its people are given a choice to convert to Islam. They are either murdered, taken as slaves, or spared depending on their decision. The army also destroys the temple in Debal.

The defeat of a king

The army then moves to the ancient cities of Nerun and Sehwan. Its people surrender with minimal casualties. Qasim also expands his army with new recruits before the final battle with Raja Dahir. The two armies clash in **712** at Ar-rur where Dahir is defeated and killed. The treasury is looted and women are taken as slaves. Qasim captures Multan, another ancient city in Pakistan. He dreams of expanding into and conquering Punjab.

The Caliph's rule

Qasim takes over the administration of the newly conquered lands and introduces *jizya*, a tax levied on permanent non-Muslim subjects in exchange for protection. There are reports to suggest that people are allowed to live and worship according to their culture. A few years later, Caliph Walid dies and Caliph Sulaiman takes his place. An arch enemy of Al-Hajjaj, Sulaiman is unable to take his revenge on Al-Hajjaj who is dead. He instead sends Qasim to Mesopotamia as a prisoner, where he is tortured and killed in **715**. Another version attributes Qasim's death to his mishandling of Raja Dahir's daughters, who were gifted to the Caliph as slaves.

150 years of Arab rule

Sindh and Multan remain under the Caliph's empire for more than 150 years. Although they are not able to make their way into mainland India, the conquest of Sindh remains an important chapter. This is the first time that a foreign power from the west succeeds in conquering and establishing its rule. This opens the doors for future invasions and leaders. It also brings Islam to India—a religion that coexists with the other religions of the subcontinent.

▼ *The Indus River is one of the most crucial water sources for the regions of Sindh and Punjab in Pakistan. It has played a significant role in the survival of several civilizations as well as for trade and commerce.*

Virupaksha Temple, Hampi

Lasting over two centuries (1336–1565), the Vijayanagar Empire signified the consolidation of political power in south India. It was founded against the backdrop of continuous invasions. The empire flourished in all areas, especially architecture. Its glory is best seen in the ruins of its capital city Hampi, in the southern state of Karnataka. Among these ruins lies the beautiful Virupaksha Temple, as seen here. Dedicated to the god Shiva, the temple was commissioned by chieftain Lakkan Dandesha under the king Deva Raya II. Its entrance tower is so striking that it can be seen from miles away.

3
THE EARLY MODERN PERIOD

1526-1858

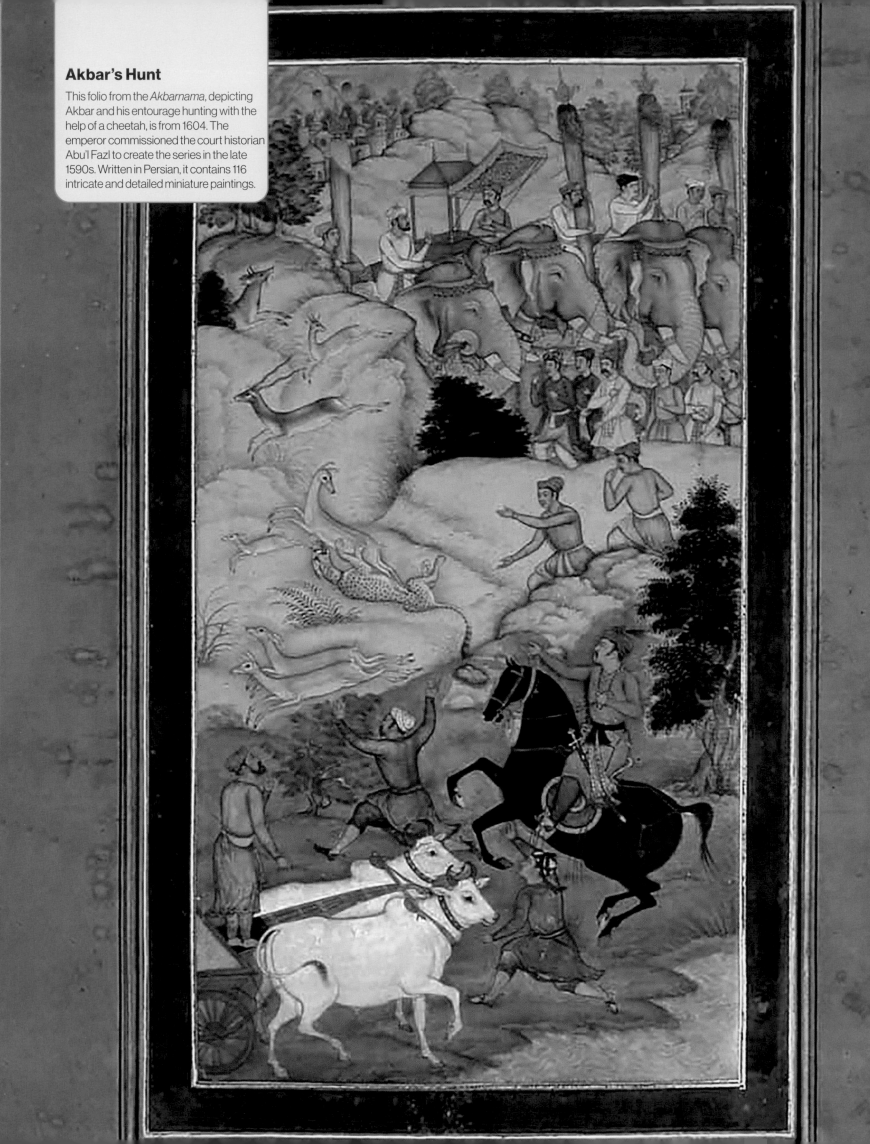

Akbar's Hunt

This folio from the *Akbarnama*, depicting Akbar and his entourage hunting with the help of a cheetah, is from 1604. The emperor commissioned the court historian Abu'l Fazl to create the series in the late 1590s. Written in Persian, it contains 116 intricate and detailed miniature paintings.

Encampment in the Hills

The *Akbarnama* was a window into life during Akbar's reign. This folio in ink, opaque watercolor, and gold on paper, depicts Akbar's son, Jehangir with a halo around his head. He is holding a falcon as his attendants look on.

Arrival of the Europeans

Indian spices were popular in Europe, but the Turkish merchants monopolized all the trade routes. This prompted European businesses to search for alternate sea routes to India. Soon, trade flourished, but that did not seem enough. They also sought control over the land.

Sir Thomas Roe
The King of England sends Sir Thomas Roe as an official ambassador to the Mughal court. He reaches Surat, Gujarat. Emperor Jehangir allows him to set up factories.

1615

Dutch factories
The Dutch East India Company sets up their first factories in Petapalli and Masulipatnam in Andhra Pradesh. They trade in cotton, indigo, silk, rice, and opium. Their influence extends east to Bengal by the mid-17th century.

c.1606

The English arrive
The British East India Company (EIC) is chartered and the English enter the scene. Victory over a Portuguese naval force in 1608 helps them establish their own outpost in Surat.

1600 ...

Goa captured
Alfonso de Albuquerque, the second Portuguese viceroy in India, captures Goa from the Sultan of Bijapur. He sets up a fortress at the port, which becomes the headquarters. By the end of the 16th century, the coasts of Daman, Diu, and Salsette Island and Bassein (Vasai) in Maharashtra, become Portuguese territories.

1510

Return
King Manuel of Portugal sends Pedro Alvares Cabral, a navigator and explorer, to establish a trading post in India. However, an uprising by local Muslim traders destroys the encampment and Cabral is forced to leave. In 1502, da Gama sets sail for India to reestablish the trading post. This time, he uses excessive force to persuade King Zamorin to sign a trade treaty.

1500

Reaching Calicut
Portuguese explorer Vasco da Gama reaches Calicut (Kozhikode) in Kerala. The first meeting with Samudri Raja or King Zamorin of Calicut is disastrous, but da Gama returns to his land with a shipload of goods that are later sold for a huge profit. He also takes back a few Indians with him, as, it is believed, hostages.

1498

Danish trade

The Danes initiate trade with India. In 1620, they obtain the port of Tranquebar (Tharangambadi) in Tamil Nadu from the Nayaks of Tanjore (Thanjavur). They follow it up with factories at Masulipatnam, Port Novo, and Serampur. However, they lack resources and are forced to sell the factories to the British and leave India in 1845.

Factory in Surat

The French East India Company sets up its first factory in Surat, Gujarat, becoming the last Europeans to set base in India. In c.1674, they obtain Pondicherry (Puducherry) from the Sultan of Bijapur and turn it into a thriving town.

Wars and conflicts

The Anglo-French War in Europe has a direct effect on India, resulting in the English clashing with the French in the three Carnatic Wars, also called the Euro-Indian Wars. Both gain footholds in their respective regions.

> **"Vasco de la Gama, a gentleman of thy house, came to my country, of whose arrival I was very glad. In my country there is abundance of cinnamon, cloves, pepper, and precious stones ... I wish to procure ... silver, gold, coral, and scarlet."**
>
> *From a letter, written by the Portuguese to the king of Portugal signed by King Zamorin, c.15th century*

1616 ...   **1668**   **1744–1763**   **1757**   **c.18th century**

Annexing territories

The outcome of the battle of Plassey solidifies British presence in India. After the battle of Buxar in 1764, the British shed their trader image. Instead, they collect revenue, maintain an army, and start annexing Indian territories.

Company rule

British forces gain monopoly over India. Their exploitative policies lead to a drain of wealth in the country as well as famines from 1770–1944, which takes a huge toll on human lives.

Looking to the world

This 164ft high (50m high) limestone monument in Lisbon, Portugal, was built to celebrate the Portuguese who made their way into the world. Featured among them is Vasco da Gama, who opened a trade route from Europe to India via the Cape of Good Hope.

Kingdoms of the South

From the mid-14th century to the 18th century, South India saw the rise and fall of many kingdoms—some big and some small. Despite their size, they made significant contributions to the political, social, and cultural life of the region. While some kingdoms were at war or swore allegiance to one another, others battled foreign powers who tried to take over their territory.

Rise of Vijayanagar

Two brothers of the Sangam dynasty, Harihara and Bukka, establish the kingdom of Vijayanagar (the city of victory). Harihara becomes the first king. The kingdom is at its greatest territorial extent, and the biggest in the south, during the reign of Krishnadeva Raya. The empire becomes known for its architectural patronage, especially for the Hampi group of monuments in Karnataka.

1336

Bahmani Sultanate

Alauddin Shah ascends the throne in north Deccan. His rule is one of peace and prosperity. The kingdom lasts for 180 years and expands across the Deccan. The Bahmanis are at odds with Vijayanagar, located further south. By the 16th century, the stronghold of the Bahmanis declines and crumbles into five states.

1347

Mysore kingdom

The Wodeyar family establishes the kingdom of Mysore. They swear allegiance to the Vijayanagar empire, till its decline. In 1565, Raja Wodeyar I declares independence. After this, Mysore undergoes steady expansion. The kingdom is consolidated during the reign of Chikka Devaraja in 1673–1744. It is during this time that it becomes a tributary state of the Mughals, with no administration curbs and interference.

1399

Deccan Sultanates

The five independent kingdoms that come up after the disintegration of the Bahmani Sultanate include Nizam Shahis of Ahmadnagar, Adil Shahis of Bijapur, Qutb Shahis of Golconda, Imad Shahis of Berar, and Barid Shahis of Bidar. The kingdoms fight each other and sometimes even join hands to defeat the common enemy.

1527

Maratha Empire

The Marathas lay the foundation of their empire, with the coronation of Shivaji, following a series of rebellions that he leads against Bijapur and the Mughals. Before this, the Deccan Sultans employed the Marathas, a warrior clan. They are a formidable force against the Mughals. However, the British challenge their power in the three Anglo-Maratha wars, which leads to their downfall.

Hyderabad State

Following Aurangzeb's death and the weakening of the Mughal state, Deccan viceroy Mir Qamar-ud-din Khan declares the region independent. He uses the titles, Asaf Jah and Nizam ul-Mulk (order of the realm) that the Mughals granted him. Seven generations of Nizams rule until the princely state merges with the Indian nation in 1947.

Mysore's new sultan

The kingdom of Mysore faces threats and begins its decline. Hyder Ali, a commander-in-chief to the Wodeyars, seizes the kingdom and becomes the sultan. His son, Tipu Sultan takes over after his death. He becomes known as the king who managed to hold off the British seeking to conquer the region.

Carnatic Sultanate

Aurangzeb creates the seat of the Nawab of Arcot for Muhammad Ismail, who helped defeat the sultans of Golconda, Bijapur, and the Marathas. After the establishment of the Deccan Sultanate, the Nawabs of Arcot swear allegiance to them.

Kingdom of Travancore

The feudal state of Venad in Kerala, becomes the kingdom of Travancore under Marthanda Varma. At its peak, the kingdom covers most of Kerala and parts of Tamil Nadu. The kingdom becomes known for defeating the Dutch East India Company at the Battle of Colachel. It later becomes a princely state under the British.

Vijayanagar's decline

A confederacy of the Deccan Sultanates overthrow the Vijayanagar Empire during the Battle of Talikota. Before this, they face threats from the Bahmani sultans. They rule for 230 years. At the end of their reign, the capital Hampi is left ravaged. The Mughals ultimately conquer the region.

1690

1724

1729

1758

1674

1565

Queens of India

Mula Gabharu
(1486–1532)

The Mughal armies tried to conquer the Ahom kingdom. In turn, Mula, the warrior-princess and daughter of the Ahom king Supimphaa, called upon women and men to fight.

1486 ...
Princess Nang Mula is born into the Ahom dynasty in the Sivasagar area of Assam. When she comes of age, she marries Phrasengmung Borgohain, an Ahom military commander.

1527
Phrasengmung is killed in battle against Turbak Khan, the Mughal invader who launches several attacks on the land. Mula is forced to lead the Ahom army. Her presence inspires many women to join the war.

1532
Mula rides her elephant, Nazing, to war against the Mughal army and fights valiantly. It is believed that she fights Turbak. She dies after sustaining injuries in battle.

Rani Durgavati
(1524–1564)

The queen of Gondwana from 1550 to 1564, Durgavati repulsed several attempts at invasion, including one by the more powerful Mughal army.

1524
Durgavati is born to Keerat Pal Singh, the Rajput ruler of Gurjar Chandela. The king ensures that his daughter is trained as a warrior.

1542
She marries Dalpat Shah of the Gond dynasty. The marriage is forged to create an alliance between two kingdoms of central India — the Chandels and the Gonds. The couple have a son named Vir Narayan.

1550
After Dalpat Shah's sudden death, Durgavati takes over the reins of the kingdom in lieu of her five-year-old son.

1550–1564
As interim ruler, Durgavati shifts the capital to Chauragarh. She orders the building of several tanks and reservoirs.

1562
Akbar's *subedar* (military officer) Abdul Majid Asaf Khan, launches an attack on Durgavati's land in the hope of expanding his domain. Riding her elephant Sarman, she fights alongside her army against the Mughal forces. Injured, she dies by suicide in order to avoid capture.

Abbakka Chowta
(1525–1570s)

Warrior-queen and ruler of the city Ullal in Karnataka, Rani Abbakka, fights off the Portuguese for many years. They tried to seize the port city because of its strategic importance.

1544
Tirumala Raya, the Chowta king, crowns his niece Abbakka the queen of Ullal. She is trained in statecraft and ascends the throne as the first queen of the Tulu-speaking people.

1550 ...
The Portuguese, who control maritime trade across the Indian Ocean, demand that she pay a tribute to continue trading. Rani Abbakka pays them no heed.

1555
Angered by her defiance, the Portuguese attack her kingdom, but Abbakka successfully resists their attempts.

1556–1568
The Portuguese attack repeatedly, but Abbakka manages to thwart each and every one of them. According to folklore, she is said to have used the agnivana (fire arrow) to fight the Portuguese.

1568
Portuguese general Joao Peixoto, with a fleet of soldiers, captures Ullal. Abbakka escapes. She returns the same night with around 200 soldiers, kills the general, and regains control.

c.1570s
Betrayed by her husband, Lakshmappa Arasa Bangaraja II, the king of Banga, Abbakka loses the war against the Portuguese. She is captured and imprisoned. While in jail, she stirs up a revolt and dies while fighting, as a warrior queen.

There have been notable, daring, and formidable female rulers throughout Indian history. These women faced extreme challenges, led their people, protected their kingdoms, and warded off invaders.

Chand Bibi
(1550–1585)

Chand Bibi is known for leading the Deccan region against the Mughals. Other than a warrior, she was also a sitar player, painter, and a skilled diplomat.

1550
Sultana Khunza Humayun, wife of Sultan Hussain Nizam Shah of Ahmednagar in Maharashtra, gives birth to a daughter. Chand grows up in a court where her mother and father enjoy almost equal powers.

1550 ...
Chand is brought up unlike other women of her times. She is given the freedom to pursue sporting activities, such as hawking along with learning how to paint and play the sitar.

1565
In order to forge stronger political alliances, Chand marries Sultan Ali Adil Shah I of Bijapur. She finds equal status in his court, joins him on campaigns, and advises him on stately affairs.

1580
Adil Shah dies in battle leaving behind his nine-year-old nephew as king. Chand takes over as queen regent. Her trusted aides betray her one after the other, but she fights back and restores her position each time.

1582
Chand returns to her maiden home but is soon forced to assume regentship of her nephew, when her brother is killed in battle against the Mughals.

1595
As the Mughals turn toward the Deccan with dreams of annexing it, Chand forges alliances with neighboring states.

1599
Warring factions within the kingdom cause Chand to take a strategic decision to call a truce with the Mughals. For this, she is ultimately murdered by one of her many opponents.

Rani Karnavati
(c.1600s–1640s)

The queen of Garhwal in Uttarakhand, Rani Karnavati gained a formidable reputation for the way she dealt with her enemies. She became known as Nak-Kati-Rani or the queen who cuts off noses.

1622
King Mahipati Shah, husband of Karnavati, ascends the throne of Garhwal and shifts the capital from Dewalgarh to Srinagar in present-day Uttarakhand.

1631
The king's reign comes to an abrupt end when he dies while launching an invasion on the Kumaon region. Karnavati assumes responsibilities as queen regent in place of her seven-year-old son Prithvi Pat Shah.

1631–1640
With the help of a group of trusted generals, Karnavati implements civic changes such as setting up hydraulic constructions. This includes the Rajpur Canal of Dehradun, the earliest canal of the region.

1640
Shah Jahan, the emperor of Delhi, sends his general, Najabat Khan, to attack Garhwal with a huge army. Karnavati traps them by blocking all roads. When the Mughals beg for a truce, she lets them go, but only after chopping off their noses. Years later, her son becomes a king and continues to keep the Mughals away from Garhwal.

Velu Nachiyar
(1730–1790)

Velu Nachiyar, the first Indian queen to wage war against the British, is fondly referred to as *veeramangai* (brave girl) in Tamil.

1730
Raja Chellamuthu Vijayaragunatha Sethupathy and Rani Sakandimuthal of the kingdom of Ramnad in Tamil Nadu welcome their only child, a daughter named Velu Nachiyar.

1730–1746
No efforts are spared in training her. She grows up skilled in the art of speaking multiple languages and fighting wars on the battlefield. In 1746, she marries the prince of Sivagangai, Muthuvaduganananthur Udaiyathevar, and they have a daughter.

1772
The British Army invades Sivagangai and kills the king. Velu escapes to Dindigul with her daughter and stays in hiding for eight years.

1772–1780
The queen meets the ruler of Mysore, Haider Ali, and earns his favor. With his help, she gathers a powerful army with the intention of attacking the British.

1780
Velu arranges a suicide attack on the British army by sending her commander-in-chief Kuyili to blow up one of their arsenals. This weakens the British force drastically.

1780
Velu wins back her husband's kingdom and rules it for 10 years, before handing it over to her daughter.

Battles and Sieges

The years between 1526 and 1849 witnessed several conquests and wars across the Indian subcontinent. Some were fought between bickering kingdoms or against foreign invaders, while others were battles that the Europeans fought to gain territory on Indian soil.

Battle of Haldighati

Mughal Emperor Akbar turns his attention to the Rajputana region in Rajasthan, hoping to extend his boundaries. Maharana Pratap of Mewar refuses to submit and enters into a battle against Akbar's forces at Haldighati, a narrow mountain pass. The Rajputs are outnumbered four to one and are defeated.

First Carnatic War

The 1744 war between England and France, which was fought for control in North America, causes hostility on Indian soil. The French snatch the trading post of Madras, Fort St. David, in Tamil Nadu, from the British. It is returned to the British with the support of the Nawab of the Carnatic.

The First Battle of Panipat

Babur, the ruler of the Timurid Empire, with an army of 10,000 men clashes against Ibrahim Lodi's force of 100,000 men and 1,000 elephants. Showing great ingenuity, Babur sets up a fortress with carts and earthen ramparts, digs trenches, and makes wise use of gunpowder. He establishes the Mughal Empire after Lodi's defeat.

1526 **1527** **1576** **1612** **1739** **1746**

Battle of Karnal

Persian King Nadir Shah defeats the Mughal Emperor Muhammad Shah in Punjab, speeding up the decline of the Mughal Empire. The win is attributed to his disciplined army and strategic use of gunfire, which causes great panic among Mughal war elephants. Muhammad is captured and Delhi is ransacked.

Battle of Khanwa

The Rajputs under Mewar's Rana Sangha want to restrict Babur's territorial expansion and meet him in battle. Their warfare techniques are no match for Babur's strategic placement of ditches, foot musketeers, falconets, and mortars. The Rajputs are defeated in less than 10 hours.

Battle of Swally

The British and Portuguese trading companies get into a naval fight over the right of trade in India near Swally, a port town in Gujarat. Victory goes to the British, marking the beginning of their increasing presence in the country.

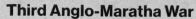

Third Anglo-Maratha War

Two wars for land acquisition are fought between the British and the Marathas. The third pits the British and Lord Hastings against the Marathas under Peshwa Baji Rao. The Marathas lose. The British annex their lands and capture the Peshwa.

Battle of Buxar

Mir Qasim, the new Nawab of Bengal, rebels and betrays the EIC. The EIC retaliates, a war follows, and Mir Qasim is defeated. He escapes to the north, forms new alliances with the Mughals, and attacks the British in Buxar, in present-day Bihar. He is defeated again.

1817 1849

1757 1764

> "In truth, each one of those famous elephants was capable of disordering a large force ... the horses had never seen such terrific forms."
>
> *Abu'l Fazl, 16th-century author, on the First Battle of Panipat, Akbarnama*

Battle of Gujrat

The battle between the Sikh army of Raja Sher Singh and the British Indian Army at Gujrat, Pakistan, leads to the annexation of Punjab. British artillery proves disastrous against the guns that the Sikh army use, and they surrender. This war is called the Battle of Guns, as the British had never seized so many guns and men in a battle before this.

Fort St. David

In the early 18th century, the British East India Company began strengthening its fortifications. By 1746, Fort St. David in Cuddalore, Tamil Nadu, became a center for the British in the southern part of India. Over the next few years, it became key as aggressions against the French adversaries became more frequent during the Carnatic wars. However, the Fort was abandoned as soon as the French were out of the picture.

Battle of Plassey

The British East India Company (EIC) starts exploiting its trading rights in Bengal. They meet Nawab Siraj-ud-Daulah of Bengal on the battleground at Plassey. The Nawab is betrayed by his own and is defeated, captured, and killed. The British establish their rule in Bengal.

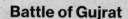

The Story of Indian Laborers

The British East India Company (EIC) used Indians as forced agricultural labor across colonies to build basic infrastructure. Though slavery had been abolished, the colonizers required people to work on their fields or to build infrastructure in their colonies. For this purpose, around 1.3 million Indian laborers were taken to work in the Caribbean region and at the Indian Ocean sugar plantations.

1833

Abolition of slavery
The British Parliament abolishes slavery in their colonies. With newly freed people, there is no one to work in the plantations. Now that they are free, the locals refuse to work under poor conditions. This is harmful for the economic interests of the British as the sugar industry is staple for them.

1834–1837

Mauritius
The EIC rebrands abolished slavery as "indentured labor." Instead, Indians sign contracts to work at plantations for a few years at a fixed daily wage. Seven thousand laborers are sent from Calcutta (Kolkata). Their destination is Mauritius in the Indian Ocean, which has sugar cane plantations.

1838

South America
A group of 396 laborers from Bhojpur in Bihar and Awadh in Uttar Pradesh are taken from Calcutta to Guyana in South America. Over the next 80 years, 230,000 more laborers are sent to Guyana.

1845

West Indies
Fatel Razakh is the first ship to take Indian indentured labor from Calcutta to Trinidad in the West Indies. It is a small ship, carrying 227 laborers, 22 children, and six infants. In 1856, the average death rate of Indians while on the ship is 17 percent, because of unsanitary conditions on board. They die of dysentery, cholera, and measles.

"... every one would leave if there was a land journey; not one would advise any of their friends to go there."

Bibee Zuhoorun, an Indian female indentured laborer's account from Mauritius, 1839

Health care

The British government begins to receive complaints of poor living conditions at plantations. An ordinance is passed, making it necessary for a doctor to certify that average medical and living accommodations at estates are available for the migrants.

Space per passenger

To avoid deaths of migrant workers in transit because of overcrowding in small ships, the designated space per passenger is increased to ensure better health. A surgeon-superintendent is also deployed on the ships to check the health of the passengers during the journey.

Natal Indian Congress

Mohandas K. Gandhi forms the Natal Indian Congress in South Africa. Its aim is to fight the discrimination migrant laborers and people of Indian origin face from the locals.

The life of an indentured laborer

Migrant workers lived in squalid conditions in plantations. They were also at the receiving end of abhorrent treatment at the hands of the British. They were confined within plantations and were denied wages if they refused to work. The EIC justified the use of indentured laborers and believed that they had protected Indians from starvation and death in their home countries. They explained that many workers were already deprived in their own country. However, in testimonies, laborers confessed that they were beaten on the voyages, assaulted, overworked, and confined in unsanitary living conditions.

1820–1879

Begum Haz? Mahal

Leads the armies of ? at Shahjahanpu? Begum Hazrat takes ? of Awadh in place ? 12-year-old son, aft? British annex it and ? her husband. She lea? rebel forces from A? seizes Lucknow, and ? her son as the ruler. S? joins forces with Nan? at the battle of Shahja?

1857   1860   1864   1879   1894   1910 ...   1917 ...

South Africa

The ship *Truro* takes indentured laborers from Madras (Chennai) to Natal in South Africa. While most laborers work at sugar cane plantations, some are employed as coal miners and railroad workers. By 1910, 200,000 Indians live in Natal.

Fiji

Leonidas, the first ship of labor to Fiji in the South Pacific Ocean, reaches with 463 Indians from Calcutta. By 1916, 87 voyages were made between India and Fiji. The migrant labor workers are called *girmitiyas*, a term derived from *girmit*, the word for agreement. Some were even called *Jahajhis*, as they were taken via *jahaj* (ship).

Gopal Krishna Gokhale

Indentured migration to Natal is put to an end following a resolution in the Imperial Legislative Council, which political leader and social reformer Gopal Krishna Gokhale proposes. He further recommends the complete prohibition of indentured labor in all the plantations.

Return to India

The British government abolishes the system of indentured labor. It comes to an end in 1920, as migrants begin returning to India. The last ship carrying returning emigrants leaves the West Indies for India in 1954. This marks the end of colonial rule over Indian lives several years after their exit from India.

British Guiana

This illustration is an artist's impression of female migrants from Calcutta as they arrive in British Guiana (Guyana) on a ship to work on sugar cane plantations. As per records only around 75,000 of them returned to India. Today, Indo-Guyanese people make up almost 40 percent of the country's population.

A F
The Rev
out acro
commor
did not s
first war

1

Ku
Leads th
The 80-year-
leads the rev
rebels in Da
district hea
escapes to Lu
Azamgarh. Wl
re

Nonconformists of the 19th century

Socio-religious movements and reformers were instrumental in uplifting many communities, breaking stereotypes, and transforming social fabric.

Jyotirao Phule (1827–1890)
Social reformer and thinker, Phule led the anti-caste movement with his wife Savitribai. He fought for equal rights, promoted education as he believed it was crucial for change, and was instrumental in setting up schools for girls and Dalit children.

Tarabai Shinde (1850–1910)
Shinde wrote *Stripurush Tulana*, one of the earliest Indian texts that challenges men's superiority. She is a legendary figure within Indian feminism for fighting for women's rights and a close associate of Savitribai Phule.

Swami Vivekananda (1863–1902)
Narendranath Datta, popularly known as Swami Vivekananda, is an Indian social reformer from Bengal, who lent his voice against caste-and-religion-based discrimination. He believed in the importance of education.

Annabhau Sathe (1920–1969)
A Dalit, born into the musical Mang community, Tukaram Bhaurao Sathe, is known for pushing past the limitations of his underprivileged background and becoming a writer. Known as the founding father of Dalit literature, his literary works in Marathi challenge discrimination on the basis of caste.

Dealing with hostility
The school, a first of its kind, angers their conservative neighbors. Jyotirao's father, Govindrao, is boycotted by the people of his own community. This forces him to ask his son and daughter-in-law to either stop their social activities or leave the house. They choose to leave.

Teachers' training
After being tutored by her husband, Savitribai joins Mrs. Mitchell's Normal School in Pune, Maharashtra. Soon, she moves to Farar's Institution in Ahmednagar and begins formal training as a teacher.

A school for girls
With Jyotirao's help, Savitribai opens a school for girls in Pune, providing free education. They start with nine students, most of whom are from underprivileged families. They teach them modern subjects, instead of the traditional Vedas taught by Brahmin teachers.

Marriage of equals
At the age of nine, she is married to Jyotirao Phule—then 13-years-old, from the same community. Child marriage is a norm at this time. Jyotirao, a supporter of women's education begins educating Savitribai.

Childhood
Daughters are not encouraged to study, especially if they are of a lower caste or Dalit. So, Savitribai, an only daughter, stays at home to help her mother with domestic work.

Birth
In Naigaon, a small village in Maharashtra, Savitribai Phule is born to Lakshmi and Khandoji Neveshe Patil. They are from the Mali community, a lower caste group associated with gardening and vegetable farming.

1849

January 1, 1848

1846

1840

1832–1839

January 3, 1831

Savitribai Phule

One of the first Dalit feminists, Savitribai Phule (1831–1897) believed that women had the right to education and to break free of the discriminatory practices imposed upon them. This meant that she faced many obstacles from those who did not share her opinion. Men hurled abuses and threw stones and dung at her, but nothing could crush her indomitable spirit.

Determined to succeed

Nothing deters Jyotirao and Savitribai from working toward their dream of providing education to deprived people and empowering them. They open two more schools in quick succession. In 1852, the education department of the British government recognizes their educational reform work and felicitates them.

Mahila Seva Mandal

Savitribai opens the Mahila Seva Mandal to spread awareness on women's rights. She also opens a shelter for pregnant widows where they can safely deliver their children. Together with Jyotirao, she lends support to widow remarriage, inter-caste marriage, and civil marriages without a Brahmin presiding over the ceremony. The couple adopts a boy born to a widow and names him Yashwant.

Literary work

Savitribai publishes Kavya Phule, a book of poetry. She pens several books throughout her life. In 1870, a series of famines hit Maharashtra. The Phules take up relief work by setting up free hostels and helping people suffering from diseases.

A society for all

Jyotirao sets up Satyashodhak Samaj, or the Truth-seekers Society, to carry out social reforms in an organized fashion. Savitribai heads the organization's women's section.

Breaking gender stereotypes

Jyotirao dies and Savitribai performs his death rites on her own, an act that is forbidden for Hindu women even today.

Death

Savitribai and her son open a clinic to help victims of plague. When she hears of a 10-year-old boy suffering from the disease, she rushes to his home and carries him on her back to the clinic. As a result, she contracts the infectious disease and dies.

1849 ...

1852 ...

1854

September 24, 1873

November 1890

March 10, 1897

> "Awake, arise, and educate, smash traditions—liberate."
>
> *Savitribai Phule, Kavya Phule, 1854*

JALLIANWALA BAGH MASSACRE

Slaughter on Baisakhi

On April 13, 1919, 90 soldiers under General Reginald Dyer's command gathered at the only entrance of a high-walled park and fired into a crowd of about 10,000 men, women, and children. They killed and injured hundreds of Indians. This deliberate massacre sparked off the first large-scale, nonviolent protest in India, known as the Noncooperation Movement.

The Rowlatt Act

World War I comes to an end in **1918**. As Britain celebrates its victory, India waits for news that it will be granted more autonomy. Soon, the Government of India Act of 1919 is passed to introduce self-governance, but the Indian National Congress (INC) leaders are unhappy as the Act is limited in its scope. Protests break out and then in **March 1919**, the British government in India passes the Rowlatt Act. This gives the British government the power to arrest or detain people indefinitely without a warrant.

Growing agitation

With Mohandas K. Gandhi at the helm, wide-scale protests take place across the country. Gandhi calls for *hartal* (strike) on **April 6, 1919**. People stop working and close their businesses and shops. Some observe 24-hour fasts in protest. Protesters gather in public spaces peacefully to create awareness against what they call "the black bills." The British government meets them with force and the police terrorize them. There are reports of protesters being shot in Delhi, Lahore, and Amritsar. Punjab faces the brunt with the most extreme of responses. Soon, Gandhi leaves Bombay to join the protests in Punjab but is not allowed to enter the state and is arrested. This angers people

even more. Peaceful demonstrations continue and are again met with police brutality. Leaders are heard warning the protesters, "Do not injure anyone but be ready to be injured." Cries of Hindu-Muslim-Sikh unity are heard as well.

Massacre in the park

On **April 13, 1919**, people in Punjab get ready to celebrate Baisakhi, a harvest festival. A number of men, women, and children gather at Jallianwala Bagh—a park closed on all sides with a small gate serving as an entrance. There are conflicting reports suggesting that the crowd has gathered to protest. General Reginald Dyer, a British officer, arrives with around 90 soldiers. His aim is to disrupt the gathering and intimidate the people. The soldiers stand at the entrance, blocking it so that no one can escape. Dyer then orders them to open fire without any prior warning until the soldiers are out of ammunition. Estimates place the number of people dead and injured that day as anywhere between 400 to 1,500.

The aftermath

Martial law is declared in Punjab. Protesters are tortured and jailed and newspapers are banned. Poet Rabindranath Tagore returns his knighthood and Gandhi launches the Noncooperation Movement.

The Hunter Commission

In **October 1919**, the Hunter Commission investigates the massacre and submits its report on **May 26, 1920**. The Commission reprimands Dyer and notes that he should have warned the gathering before firing. However, it declares that the imposition of martial law in Punjab was justified. In Britain, reactions to the massacre are divided. Some, such as British politician Winston Churchill, condemn the act, while others laud Dyer, who is later awarded a sword by the House of Lords. It carries the inscription "Saviour of the Punjab."

Impact on the freedom movement

The massacre has a profound impact on the freedom movement, driving young men and women to join the struggle for independence. In London, on **March 13, 1940**, Udham Singh, a revolutionary, shoots and kills Sir Michael O'Dwyer, who had ordered the massacre. Singh is captured, jailed, and executed.

100 Years later

In **2019**, on its 100th anniversary, the Jallianwala Bagh massacre becomes a subject of debate in the British Parliament. The British Prime Minister Theresa May shares her regret over the incident as well.

"The darkest stain on British rule in India"
A headline in The Leader, Allahabad, 1919

The walls that speak

Post Independence, the massacre site at Jallianwala Bagh in Amritsar, Punjab, has been preserved as a memorial. The bullet holes, outlined in white, can still be seen on the walls.

1917

"I am not against one nation in particular, but against the general idea of all nations."

In the essay, "On Nationalism In India," 1912
With his growing involvement in the Indian freedom struggle, Rabindranath becomes interested in the idea of nationhood. His main aim is to promote the idea of a single nest without boundaries. For him, human bonds are more important than national boundaries.

1913

"Where the mind is without fear and the head is held high ... into that heaven of freedom my father let my country awake."

Gitanjali, 1912
Rabindranath wins the Nobel prize in Literature in 1913 for *Gitanjali*, a book of poetry. He is the first Asian and Indian to win the prestigious award. Two years later, the British award him the knighthood in recognition of his literary contributions.

1919

"I for my part, wish to stand, shorn of all special distinctions, by the side of my countrymen who, for their so-called insignificance, are liable to suffer a degradation not fit for human beings....."

From a letter to the Viceroy of India, 1919
General Reginald Dyer opens fire on a peaceful gathering at Jallianwala Bagh in Amritsar. Close to 400 people are killed and thousands injured. This act of mindless butchering agonizes Rabindranath, and he returns his knighthood as a form of protest.

1878–1932

"... there is no other way to enforce our right to establish contact with God simultaneously through knowledge, love and service, except through humanity."

Builders of Modern India: Rabindranath Tagore, 1971
Rabindranath travels to almost 30 countries, delivering lectures and forging ties. He tells the people of these countries about India and also enriches himself with valuable ideas from his hosts. Over time, he develops an

1905

"What is needed is eagerness of heart for a fruitful communication between different cultures. Anything that prevents this is barbarism."

The Philosophy of Rabindranath Tagore, 2005
Lord Curzon issues an order to partition Bengal into two parts on the basis of religion. Rabindranath is greatly aggrieved. He gives a call for boycotting foreign goods and starts the Rakhi Utsav to celebrate intercommunal harmony.

1901

"Universities should never be made into mechanical organizations for collecting and distributing knowledge."

Creative Unity, 1926
Rabindranath establishes a residential school in Santiniketan, Bolpur, where classes happen in open air. His aim is to take education beyond the four walls of the classroom. The first session has five students. In 1921, the school is expanded and becomes the Visva-Bharati University.

Rabindranath Tagore

Poet, writer, composer, playwright, painter, and Nobel Laureate, Rabindranath Tagore (1861–1941) was one of the most prolific minds of the 20th century and counted as one of the foremost Indian thinkers and educators of his time. His contribution to India's freedom movement and the world of literature remains immeasurable.

1861

"For, under this system [of school education], the child is separated from the bosom of nature and society and placed in the factory that goes by the name of school."

An observation by Rabindranath Tagore

Rabindranath is born into a prominent and privileged Bengali household to social reformer Debendranath Tagore and Sarada Devi. He has an unusual childhood. His mother dies early, and he is brought up by the household staff. He does not like formal education and is mostly home-schooled. Rabindranath composes his first set of verses at the age of eight.

1941

"I have given ... whatever I had to give. In return if I receive anything—some love, some forgiveness—then I will take it with me when I step on the boat that crosses to the festival of the wordless end...."

Last poem dictated by him, 1941

Rabindranath suffers two long bouts of illness toward the later stages of his life. He does not fully recover and dies, at the age of 80, on August 7 at Jorasanko, his ancestral home in present-day Kolkata.

uneasy relationship with mainstream Indian politics and leaders, such as Mohandas K. Gandhi. He c continues to stress on the power of humanity and spirituality in the path of attaining freedom, not just for the nation but for oneself.

Voices of the Freedom Movement

The struggle for Independence began with the early nationalists or moderates. Their emergence in the late 19th century marked the beginning of an organized movement when they protested peacefully, wrote articles in newspapers, and relied on political reach. Many went on to hold key positions in independent India.

Sarojini Naidu

Sarojini Naidu (1879–1949), also known as the "nightingale of India," is drawn to the INC and the freedom movement while living in Britain where she is working on women's rights. She travels across India from 1915 to 1918, giving lectures on social welfare and nationalism. She becomes the first Indian woman president of the INC in 1925 and is at the forefront of several key movements. She is appointed governor of the United Provinces (Uttar Pradesh) in Independent India, becoming the first woman to hold such a post.

G Subramania Iyer

A journalist, G Subramania Iyer (1855–1916) launches *The Hindu*, a weekly newspaper with five others in Madras, Tamil Nadu. As editor, he writes against British-controlled press propaganda. He also starts the Tamil newspaper *Swadesamitran* in 1882, where he writes against the British and supports the Indian National Congress (INC).

> **"The nations that in fettered darkness weep
> Crave thee to lead them where great mornings break …
> Mother, O Mother, wherefore dost thou sleep
> Arise and answer for thy children's sake!"**
>
> *Sarojini Naidu, in her poem "To India"*, **The Golden Threshold, 1905**

1878	1892	1902	1904...	1905

Dadabhai Naoroji

Scholar and industrialist Dadabhai Naoroji (1825–1917) is elected to the British Parliament. One of the founding members of the INC, he is known as the "grand old man of India." He uses his position in Parliament and his writings in *Poverty and Un-British Rule in India*, to criticize British economic policies that are draining India of its wealth.

> **"I think all fair-minded persons will have to admit that it is absolutely monstrous that a class of human beings, with bodies similar to our own … should be perpetually condemned to a low life of … servitude and mental and moral degradation."**
>
> *Gopal Krishna Gokhale, in a speech, 1903*

Bhikaiji Cama

Political activist Bhikaiji Cama (1861–1936) leaves India and moves to London for medical treatments. Here, she spends her time working toward gathering international support against British rule in India. In 1922, she unfurls an early version of the Indian tricolor flag at the International Socialist Congress in Stuttgart, Germany. She also helps launch the revolutionary newspaper *Bande Mataram*.

> **"When India is independent, women will not only have the right to vote but all other rights."**
>
> *Bhikaiji Cama, c.20th century*

> **"… there was a … drain of wealth … Europeans … seized them [riches] in defiance of all economic principles."**
>
> *Dadabhai Naoroji, 1901*

Gopal Krishna Gokhale

Social worker and a professor, Gopal Krishna Gokhale (1866–1915) leaves his job to enter politics and join the freedom movement. He criticizes land revenue systems and plays an important role in framing the Morley-Minto reforms of 1909, which increase Indian participation in governance. He advocates the rights of the backward classes and later becomes Mohandas K. Gandhi's mentor.

Kazi Nazrul Islam

At 17, Kazi Nazrul Islam (1899–1976), Bengali poet and revolutionary, becomes a journalist, sometime after he leaves the British Army during World War I. He writes revolutionary poetry criticizing the British alongside articles in his magazine, *Dhumketu*. His writings, promoting secularism, lead to his frequent imprisonment. Today, he is celebrated as the national poet of Bangladesh.

Abul Kalam Azad

Abul Kalam Azad (1888–1958), through his Urdu newspaper *Al-Hilal*, comes into the spotlight with his scathing critique of the British. Authorities soon ban the publication. Azad opposes the Partition and as a scholar of Islam promotes Hindu-Muslim unity. He is active during the Civil Disobedience and Khilafat movements. In 1947, he becomes the first minister of education and helps establish Indian Institutes of Technology across India.

> "Come brother Hindu! Come Musalman! Come Buddhist! Come Christian! Let us transcend all barriers, let us forsake forever all smallness, all lies, all selfishness and let us call brothers as brothers. We shall quarrel no more."
>
> ***Kazi Nazrul Islam in an editorial
> Joog Bani, 1920***

Motilal Nehru

Lawyer Motilal Nehru (1861–1931) becomes President of the INC. He forms the Swaraj Party in 1923 to obstruct the functioning of the British government. He later releases the Nehru Report in 1928 to demand dominion status for India. This is in response to the Simon Commission, which is set up to assess constitutional reform in India.

1912	1916	1917	c.1917–1918	1919	1928

> "We cannot succeed in anything if we act in fear of other people's opinions."
>
> ***C Rajagopalachari, c. 20th century***

Abdul Gaffar Khan

Pashtun leader Abdul Gaffar Khan (1890–1988) leads the protests against the Rowlatt Act in the North-West Frontier Province. He promotes nonviolent resistance and forms the Khudai Khidmatgar, against colonial rule among Pashtuns. He is called "Frontier Gandhi" for following Gandhian philosophy.

C Rajagopalachari

After an encounter with Gandhi, C Rajagopalachari (1878–1972) gives up law and joins the struggle for independence. From 1912 to 1941, he is imprisoned five times for his role in the different movements. Also known as Rajaji, he serves as the chief minister of the Madras Presidency from 1952 to 1954.

> "... twin of patience."
>
> ***Abdul Gaffar Khan, describing nonviolence, c.20th century***

Annie Besant

British social reformer and educationalist, Annie Besant (1847–1933) launches the Indian Home Rule Movement with activist Bal Gangadhar Tilak. They campaign for democracy and dominion status in India. In 1917, she becomes the first woman president of the INC. She works against casteism and child marriages. She is one of the founders of the Banaras Hindu University.

> "Take to the path of dharma—the path of truth and justice. Don't misuse your valor. Remain united."
>
> ***Sardar Vallabhbhai Patel, in a speech c.1918***

Sardar Vallabhbhai Patel

Sardar Patel (1875–1950) rises to prominence after successfully leading the peasants in the Bardoli Satyagraha in Gujarat against increased taxes. Also known as the "iron man of India," he is the country's first home minister and convinces almost every princely state to join India after Independence.

The Freedom Struggle

India saw several protests and uprisings even before the Revolt of 1857. Yet they were often small and scattered across the country. The larger political awakening came about only in the early 1900s with the emergence of cohesive mass movements and iconic leaders. India's struggle for independence finally came to an end in 1947 when the British left the country.

Indigo Revolt

Thousands of indigo farmers in Bengal's Nadia district rise up against the British. They have been forced to cultivate indigo instead of food crops and work on disadvantageous terms. They refuse to grow indigo and go on a peaceful strike but are soon overpowered and slaughtered.

The Munda Rebellion

Around the Chotanagpur region, the Mundas rise up in rebellion under the leadership of Birsa Munda. They try to reclaim the lands that the British have taken from them.

Champaran Satyagraha

The peasants of Champaran, Bihar, launch a satyagraha (truth-force) under Gandhi's guidance in protest against the British policy that is forcing them to sell indigo at very low prices. Gandhi develops satyagraha as a form of nonviolent resistance.

Noncooperation Movement

In response to the Jallianwala Bagh massacre in Amritsar, Gandhi demands Swaraj (self-rule) for India. He uses the path of satyagraha for this. Despite its peaceful intentions, the campaign turns violent, when a group of protesters clashes with the police in Chauri Chaura, Uttar Pradesh. This results in the death of 22 policemen and three civilians. Gandhi suspends the movement.

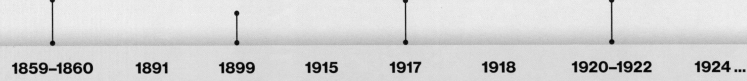

1859–1860   **1891**   **1899**   **1915**   **1917**   **1918**   **1920–1922**   **1924 ...**

Anglo–Manipur War

An armed struggle breaks out when the British empire tries to take advantage of royal disputes in the Kingdom of Manipur. This is so that they can gain ownership over Manipur. The Manipuris put up a strong front but are subdued, and the British take direct control of the region.

Kheda Satyagraha

The peasants at Kheda in Gujarat protest against the British government's policy of extracting taxes in the region despite the failure of crops. Gandhi lends his support.

Gandhi's campaigns

After two years in prison for sedition, Gandhi returns to campaign for Swaraj. He leads the Dandi March in 1930, against the British-imposed salt tax. The act sparks civil disobedience movements across the country.

First national campaign

Mohandas K. Gandhi begins to campaign for the INC. In 1919, the British introduce the Rowlatt Act, allowing indefinite detention of political agitators. Gandhi orders a *hartal* (strike), shutting shops and businesses as a form of civil disobedience.

Early uprisings

Before the Revolt of 1857, many rebellions took place against the British. Though smaller in scale, these left an indelible mark in India's history.

1760–1800 Muslim and Hindu monks in Bengal rise up against the British government that takes away their right to collect alms during pilgrimage. They take up banditry in retaliation.

1806 A new sepoy dress code is implemented in Vellore, Tamil Nadu. Hindus are prohibited from wearing religious marks and Muslims have to shave their beard. Soldiers protest but face court martial as a result.

Waiting for freedom

Some of the key leaders of the freedom struggle included (clockwise from left, in the foreground) Jawaharlal Nehru, Pashtun leader Khan Abdul Gaffar Khan, Vallabhbhai Patel, Maulana Abul Kalam Azad, and Mohandas K. Gandhi. They are seen here at an All India Congress Committee meeting in 1947.

1928

1942–1945

1946

Bardoli Satyagraha

Despite a decline in cotton prices, the British government hikes taxes. This puts immense pressure on Gujarat's peasants, already reeling from the effects of famines and floods in the previous years. Vallabhbhai Patel leads 80,000 villagers who refuse to pay the taxes. British forces make mass arrests and confiscate lands. The satyagraha continues and taxes are reduced. Gandhi gives Patel the title of Sardar for his exceptional leadership.

Quit India Movement

Gandhi opposes the British using Indian soldiers to fight World War II. He believes that India cannot fight for the freedom of others while they are being denied their freedom. The British send Stafford Cripps to negotiate India's support to the war in return for more power for the INC. Gandhi, in response, launches the Quit India Movement, which demands complete independence.

Indian Navy mutiny of 1946

Indian sailors from Bombay (Mumbai) go on a hunger strike protesting against the unfair treatment and living conditions of Indians in the navy. The movement gains traction as large numbers join in support. It gradually takes on a nationalistic character with the demand for independence from British rule becoming the larger agenda.

THE 16TH-CENTURY VELLORE FORT, IN VELLORE CITY, TAMIL NADU

1812 The Kurichiyas, a tribal group from the Wayanad region of Kerala ,attack police stations after the British encroach upon their territory.

1829–1833 After gaining ownership over land in the northeast, the British plan on building a road through the Khasi hills. This angers the Khasis, who lead a four-year agitation against them.

1855 British disrupt lives of the Santhals in Jharkhand through the introduction of the Zamindari system in their region, who in turn, launch an attack on them.

AFTER

The British decided to leave India following World War II, and prepared for a transfer of power. However, there were differences as the INC wanted complete independence and the Muslim League, a separate nation. In February 1946, the Cabinet Mission granted India its dominion status. The Muslim League objected and announced a nationwide protest, which ended in communal violence. Finally, in 1947, the Viceroy of India, Lord Mountbatten's Independence Act divided the land into two countries—India and Pakistan.

PARTITION OF INDIA

A country divided

In August 1947, the British withdrew, handing over the reins of power to Indians after 200 years of rule. The joy of a hard-fought independence brought with it a country torn and divided by religion. As the new nations—India and Pakistan—struggled to come to terms with their new borders, their people were forced to begin the arduous process of leaving their homes. This led to one of the largest migrations in human history. What followed was large-scale violence that left 200,000 to 2 million dead and displaced 10 to 20 million people.

Freedom on the horizon

World War II begins in **1939**. Britain drags India into it without consulting its leaders, who are furious. Indian National Congress (INC) demands complete independence at the end of the war but are ignored. Protests rage through India. The Muslim League extends its support to the British. They demand a separate country for Muslims at their annual session in **1940**. The British government tries to pacify the Indians and win their support during the war. They send Sir Stafford Cripps, a minister, in the spring of **1942**, with a proposal. According to it, India will be allowed self-governance while staying within the British Crown. INC rejects it and launches the Quit India Movement.

Beginning of the end

Britain decides to withdraw from India after the end of World War II in **1945**. A three-member Cabinet Mission is organized to formulate the Independence Plan in **1946**. They propose an interim government headed by Jawaharlal Nehru, and a Constituent Assembly to frame the Indian Constitution. The Muslim League opposes this.

A plan to divide

Lord Mountbatten, the new Viceroy of India, arrives in **February 1947**. He presents the Indian Independence Act, 1947, which includes dividing India into two dominions. The princely states are given the choice of joining any one of the two countries. Cyril Radcliffe, a lawyer with no knowledge of the terrain of the subcontinent, is given the impossible task of drawing the borderlines on undivided India. He is given 36 days to do this. In **July 1947**, the Boundary Commission, chaired by Radcliffe, proposes a mandate to keep Hindu and Muslim communities within the territories of India and Pakistan.

Rising tensions

With the country now divided on communal lines, Hindu–Muslim riots erupt across India. Neighbors that once coexisted peacefully turn against each other. The regions of Punjab, Bihar, and Bengal are the most affected with unspeakable violence leaving countless dead and homeless in its trail. Mohandas K. Gandhi vows to fast until death unless these killings end.

Independence

The British exit, leaving behind two countries that are irrevocably split. Pakistan celebrates its independence on **August 14, 1947,** and India, the next day, on **August 15, 1947**. However, this moment of celebration, of hard-fought independence, turns disastrous.

The violence of Partition

Millions of people are forced to flee their homes and make the journey to their new country. They use any means they have—on foot, by bullock carts, trains, and on train roofs. In Punjab, Muslims move from East Punjab to the West, to what is now Pakistan, while Hindus and Sikhs travel in the opposite direction toward India. Similar movements are seen in Bengal with the creation of East Bengal, the Sindh region of Pakistan, Gujarat, Delhi, and the Princely States of Jammu and Kashmir. On the way, properties are lost and families are separated. Violence breaks out between different communities, leaving a trail of death and destruction. Whole trains pull into stations carrying bodies of people who have been slaughtered. Many people end up in refugee camps, living in squalid conditions and dying from disease and hunger.

A dark legacy

The implications of Partition as a political solution to settle religious conflict are felt in communities to this day. People continue to discuss how Partition has affected their families and the trauma that has impacted generations of Indians and Pakistanis.

"Hindustan had become free. Pakistan had become independent ... but man was still ... slave of prejudice ... slave of religious fanaticism ... slave of barbarity."

Saadat Hasan Manto, writer, 1947

A new home
Refugees wait for protected transportation as they get ready to leave for Pakistan. This became a common sight, as news of Partition broke and mass migrations began.

FIRST GENERAL ELECTIONS

A festival of democracy

From October 25, 1951, to February 21, 1952, every corner of India saw long lines of voters who inched their way to election booths to cast their vote. This was a historic moment for a young, newly independent India. With more than 15,000 candidates, conducting free and fair elections for 173,200,000 voters was a mammoth and complicated yet grand affair.

Preparing electoral rolls

As India embarks on its first elections after Independence, one important thing is missing—the electoral rolls with the electorate count. The experience of the elections in **1937** and **1942** under the Government of India Act, 1935, does not count as then limited people had voting rights. The census reports since **1881** prove useless as well, furnishing only numbers and no voter list. A door-to-door survey is commissioned. Almost 16,500 clerks work day and night to type out the electoral rolls. Eventually, 173,200,000 people are determined as eligible voters—citizens over the age of 21. In **1988**, the electoral age is amended to 18 years.

Party symbols

The literacy rate of 18 percent proves to be a challenge. It is not possible to have ballot papers with party names written down. A creative decision is taken to replace letters with symbols. Taken from everyday life in India, these symbols represent the different political parties. The Indian National Congress (INC) picks the symbol of a pair of bullocks carrying a yoke, while the Forward Bloc (Ruikar Group) opts for the hand symbol. Years later, the INC becomes synonymous with the hand symbol.

The ballot boxes

Soon, another problem arises. There is a requirement for a safe and secure box for the ballot papers. With a total of 224,000 polling booths and each candidate needing a separate box, the number of ballot boxes required comes to almost 1.2 million. The limited time and resources make it seem like an impossible task. Nathalal Panchal—a worker employed with Godrej, a company that manufactures locks and lockers—comes to the rescue. He provides the blueprint of a box that is sturdy, safe, and budget-friendly. The manufacture of the ballot boxes begins in the second half of **1951**. Employees work nonstop and pull extra shifts. Godrej accomplishes the task in months and just in time for the elections.

The first voter

The first state to have its elections is Himachal Pradesh. It takes place on **October 25, 1951**, five months before the rest of the country, to avoid the extreme winter months. Kalpa's Shyam Saran Negi, a teacher by profession, is assigned polling duty. He requests the polling officer to let him cast his vote before assuming his election role. The officer agrees and Negi makes history as the first voter of independent India.

Polling begins

The polling is held in phases over the next five months. Different parts of the country are assigned specific dates. The voting starts from **October 25, 1951,** and continues till **February 21, 1952**. Sukumar Sen, India's first Election Commissioner, oversees the entire process. Around 45 percent of voters above the age of 21 turn up to cast their vote.

The results

Of the 53 contesting parties, the INC, also the ruling party, is considered one of the strongest contenders. There is strong opposition as well with Bharatiya Jana Sangh under Syama Prasad Mukherjee, the Scheduled Caste Federation under Dr. BR Ambedkar, the Kisan Mazdoor Praja Party under JB Kripalani, and the Socialist Party under Ram Manohar Lohia and Jayaprakash Narayan. INC wins 74 percent of the seats and is declared the ruling party.

Communalism

Records trace violence along communal lines to pre-independent, early 18th-century India. Initially few and far between, the cases increased toward the second half of the 20th century. Religious animosity, ethnic conflict, and marginalization were just some of the reasons why communal tensions often laid siege to India. There is no denying that each riot—big or small—has been a dark chapter in the history of contemporary India.

February 1961
Jabalpur, Madhya Pradesh

In what is perhaps the first major incident of communal violence in post-Partition India, riots break out between Hindus and Muslims over reports of an alleged rape. Violence spills into nearby towns as well with a mounting death toll and extensive destruction of property. Soon after, Prime Minister Jawaharlal Nehru forms the National Integration Council, which aims to look at ways to promote communal harmony and combat communalism, casteism, and regionalism.

September 1969
Gujarat

A slew of socioeconomic and political factors lead to a series of communal clashes in Ahmedabad and the surrounding areas. Official figures indicate that 660 people from both the communities are killed, with more than a 1,000 injured, and properties worth millions destroyed.

February 1983
Nellie, Assam

A violent and armed mob surrounds Nellie and 13 other villages. In a little over six hours, they kill 1,800 immigrants. The massacre takes place at a time when locals view the Bangladeshi immigrants living in rural Assam as "outsiders." Things come to a head when the immigrants are given the right to vote in the local assembly elections.

October–November 1984
Delhi

The assassination of Prime Minister Indira Gandhi by her Sikh bodyguards amid the separatist movement in Punjab rouses anti-Sikh sentiments. Armed mobs take over Delhi. They set gurudwaras and Sikh neighborhoods on fire and massacre Sikh women, men, and children. More than 3,000 Sikhs are murdered.

May 1987
Meerut and Hashimpura, Uttar Pradesh

Meerut has a deep-rooted history of conflict between the Hindu and Muslim communities. In 1987, following developments in the Babri Masjid dispute, protests break out, leading to large-scale violence that shatters the trust between the two communities. The Provincial Armed Constabulary, the state's armed police, is called in to control the violence. They pick up 50 Muslims from Hashimpura village in Meerut, take them to the outskirts of the town, shoot them, and dump their bodies in the canals nearby. Nearly three decades later, the Delhi High Court finds 16 former PAC personnel guilty and sentences them to life in prison.

October 1989
Bhagalpur, Bihar

A procession collecting donations for the Ram Temple in Ayodhya makes its way through a Muslim-dominated area in Bhagalpur and is attacked. Soon, there are rumors of attacks on both the communities. Mob violence spreads across the city. Houses and shops are torched, displacing 50,000 people and causing about 1,000 deaths.

December 1992–January 1993
Mumbai, Maharashtra

Communal tensions are at an all-time high as news of the Babri Masjid demolition trickles into the city and its suburbs. Incidents of mob violence, arson, and assault take place between December and January. Homes of Hindus and Muslims are set on fire, 900 people are stabbed or killed, and over 2,000 are injured by the time things are brought under control.

February–March 2002
Gujarat

Gujarat, a state with a legacy of communal violence, sees unprecedented mob violence and rioting in 2002. It begins when a train with Hindu pilgrims returning from Ayodhya stops in Godhra, Gujarat, and a fight breaks out between them and Muslims living in the town. A train coach catches fire, killing 58 people, including women and children. This sparks off a riot that lasts over two months. During this time, Muslim women, children, and men become targets, across the state. They are brutalized and attacked. Nearly 1,000 people, mostly Muslims, are killed.

July 2012
Assam

Violence breaks out between indigenous tribespeople, the Bodos, and the Muslims in the districts of Kokrajhar and Chirang. The riot spreads to remote fields and entire villages are burned down. More than 90 people are killed and several hundreds of thousands displaced.

2013   Muzaffarnagar, Uttar Pradesh

Historically peaceful relations between Jats, a Hindu community, and Muslims are disrupted over a suspected case of stalking. A mahapanchayat (village council) gathers where hate speeches are delivered. Violence soon breaks out leading to murders, cases of arson, and the displacement of 50,000.

January 2020
Delhi

Communal riots rage as mobs armed with rods and machetes attack mostly Muslims, destroying their homes and shops. The police are criticized for their passive response, and many families flee Delhi. The riots take place following a series of protests against the Citizenship Amendment Act, 2019. According to it, all migrants, except Muslims, who faced religious persecution in their country—were eligible for citizenship.

Movements for Change

Independent India has witnessed several instances when civilians have taken to the streets to voice their discontent with prevailing social conditions. Each movement has been unique in its composition and character, but they have all relied on nonviolent means to register civil unrest. While some gathered momentum on a national scale, others remained localized. Yet they all tell a unique story of persistence and resilience.

Anti-Arrack Movement

In Nellore, Andhra Pradesh, the deep-rooted alcoholism, created by the racket of locally made alcohol (arrack), also harms rural women. Suffering from poverty and domestic violence due to their husbands' alcoholism, the women of the region spontaneously mobilize themselves to protest against arrack trade. They picket alcohol shops and petition to prohibit the sale of arrack. Their fight leads to a change in government and a ban on arrack.

1992

Bodies as human shields

Chipko Movement was named so because *chipko* means to "embrace" or "cling to." Women led the movement as they hugged trees to protect them from loggers.

Chipko Movement

In the early 1970s, large-scale felling of trees in Uttarakhand has an adverse effect on the region's ecology. In 1973, the government allots a part of the forest in Mandal village to a sports company for logging. The villagers hug trees to prevent the loggers, and their protest is successful. A year later, women from Reni village stop a contractor from cutting trees. The movement's success leads to a 15-year ban on commercial tree felling.

Namantar Andolan

The Dalit youth in Maharashtra demand that the Marathwada University in Aurangabad be renamed after Dr. BR Ambedkar. The political parties initially accept the demands, but in 1978, the Savarna community opposes it. They commit atrocities against the Dalits. The agitation continues for two decades and concludes in 1994 when the name is changed to Dr. Babasaheb Ambedkar Marathwada University.

Movement against dowry deaths

The 1970s and 1980s witness several cases of bride murders owing to dowry demands. Many women's rights organizations, such as the Progressive Organization of Women and Dahej Virodhi Chetna Manch, agitate and call for legal reforms. Finally, the law is amended and investigation into all bride deaths within seven years of marriage is made mandatory.

Save Silent Valley

The proposal to construct a hydroelectric project on the Kunthipuzha River in Kerala leads to a surge of protests when research reveals that 1,310 acres (530 hectares) of ecologically rich forest in Silent Valley would be submerged as a consequence. A decade-long movement by environmentalists, scholars, and forest communities results in the state government calling off the project. Silent Valley is declared a national park in 1985.

1973   **1974**   **1975**   **1976**

Movement for Right to Information (RTI) Act

Rajasthan-based farmers' organization Mazdoor Kisan Shakti Sangathan raises the demand to access the government records, which, they believe, will show the misappropriation of funds. After their request is denied, they assert the citizens' right to information and launch a mass movement in Rajasthan. The movement leads to an amendment in Rajasthan's Panchayati Raj Act and takes on a national face, leading to the legislation of the RTI bill in 2005.

Narmada Bachao Andolan (NBA)

The ambitious plan of constructing multiple dams on the Narmada River at the cost of submerging 245 villages, displacing 250,000 people, and the depletion of ecological resources leads to calls to stop the construction and rehabilitate the displaced. This movement, led by social activists Medha Patkar and Baba Amte, leads to the formulation of a National Rehabilitation Policy in 2003.

Bhopal Gas Tragedy protests

An accidental gas leak from a Union Carbide pesticide plant leads to the death of thousands of people within a few hours in Bhopal, Madhya Pradesh. It is considered one of the worst industrial disasters in the world. The deaths mount over the years. A year later, the victims march through Bhopal demanding justice. The protest continues even today as victims demand a rehabilitation plan, adequate compensation, medical support, clean up of the toxic site, and the prosecution of the parties responsible.

Meira Paibi

Local women, who call themselves *Meira Paibis*, or women with torches, drive this movement in Manipur. They wield *podon* (torch) and *lalten* (lanterns) as symbols to suggest their use of light to eliminate darkness. They start an anti-liquor mass movement in the 1970s when the state is wrought with alcoholism and drug abuse. The group also protests against the Armed Forces (Special Powers) Act, which is passed to control violence in the state. They speak up against cases of disappearances, torture, and extra-judicial killings.

1990   **1988–1989**   **1984**   **1977**

India Against Corruption

Social activist Anna Hazare led the India Against Corruption movement. It uses nonviolent methods to pressurize the government to enact the Jan Lokpal Bill in order to reduce corruption. The movement sees widespread protests across 60 cities. Hazare pledges to fast unto death. Ultimately, an offshoot of the movement leads to the formation of the Aam Aadmi Party. With this, the movement takes on a political color, even as the party is electorally successful.

Nirbhaya Movement

The fatal gang rape of a physiotherapy student—symbolically identified as "Nirbhaya," meaning "one who doesn't fear"—in Delhi sparks protests. There is a demand for safer conditions for women and strict anti-rape laws. Candlelight marches and night vigils are held throughout the country. This later results in reforms in criminal law.

Campaign against acid attacks

Rising reports of acid attacks on women drives survivor Laxmi Agarwal to start campaigns against acid attacks. Her movement raises awareness and compels governments to regulate the sale of acid and amend laws for easier prosecutions of acid attackers.

Citizenship Amendment Act (CAA) protests

In December 2019, the CAA, along with the National Register of Citizens (NRC), is brought forth. These policies raise questions of religious discrimination. Protests in the form of civil disobedience, strikes, and social media activism break out across the country. Women lead an around-the-clock sit-in at Shaheen Bagh, Delhi. There are several attempts to suppress the protests, which come to an end a few months later. Their efforts, however, delay the implementation of the policies.

2011   **2012**   **2014**   **2019–2020**

POLIO-FREE INDIA

A drive for mass immunization

The eradication of polio in India has been an extraordinary model in the health and governance sector. However, what lay at its heart was not some magic of medical science. Instead, it was the unwavering commitment of millions of volunteers, who left no stone unturned in the war against polio. From train stations and religious places to construction sites and remote neighborhoods, this brigade went to unimaginable lengths to reach millions of children with the vaccine.

Challenges ahead

In the **1960s**, India is considered one of the most difficult places in the world to eliminate polio. This is because of its vast population of billions, tropical climate, poor sanitation, and lack of access to health care facilities. Polio is an infectious disease that can affect the central nervous system, weaken muscles, and cause paralysis. About 60 percent of the polio cases in the world are traced to India.

A vaccine is introduced

There is a ray of hope in **1961** when Polish American scientist Dr. Albert Sabin creates the Oral Polio Vaccine (OPV). It is first used in Delhi in **1978** under a pilot program. Yet till the early **1990s**, 200,000 to 400,000 Indians continue to contract polio every year.

Commitment to complete eradication

India signs the international Global Polio Eradication Initiative led by the World Health Organization (WHO) in **1988**. It commits to the complete eradication of polio with the target of 100 percent vaccination.

Pulse Polio

On **October 2, 1994**, India begins the Pulse Polio immunization program. WHO,

Rotary International, and UNICEF aid the government in its vaccination drive. Health workers, local officials, and more than two million volunteers conduct door-to-door vaccination using OPVs. The target group in **1995** is children below three years of age, but in **1996**, the program is expanded to those below five years.

In-house production

From **1996**, the pharmaceutical company Bharat Biotech International Limited and other indigenous vaccine producers produce the polio vaccine in India. As of **2020**, several pharmaceutical companies, including Bharat Biotech, have played a crucial role in producing vaccines during the COVID-19 pandemic.

Awareness drive

By **2000**, polio vaccines succeed in eradicating polio in many parts of the world. India, however, is faced with rumors regarding vaccines offending social and religious beliefs. In **2002**, a media campaign begins to increase public awareness. Actor Amitabh Bachchan is appointed as UNICEF's polio ambassador to encourage people to embrace the vaccine. He spends the next few years personally giving OPVs to children and promoting "*do boond zindagi ki*" (two drops for life). In **2007**, the government, in order to increase vaccination coverage

in the worst-affected states of Uttar Pradesh and Bihar, begin tracking newborn babies. This is to ensure that they are given the OPV immediately. In the quest for complete coverage and access, the Indian armed forces transport vaccines to the furthest of regions, such as the mountains of the Northeast and the deserts of Rajasthan.

Eradication of polio

Finally, after years of persistence, the last polio case is reported on **January 13, 2011**, in Howrah, West Bengal. India receives its polio-free certification, along with the entire Southeast Asian region, on **March 27, 2014**. The country continues its efforts to remain polio-free, with special immunization days, booth setups, and household visits. On each National Immunization Day, an average of more than 172 million children are immunized by 2.3 million vaccinators. The World Bank calls the eradication of polio in India "one of the biggest achievements in global health."

▶ *Reaching every child*
A health worker vaccinates a child against polio with two drops of the oral polio vaccine. Volunteers visited houses across India to ensure that every child was vaccinated against the disease.

"... India proved to the world how to conquer this disease: through the strong commitment of the government, seamless partnership ... and above all the tireless hard work of millions of front-line workers."

Nicole Deutsch, head of polio operations for UNICEF in India, to the BBC, 2014

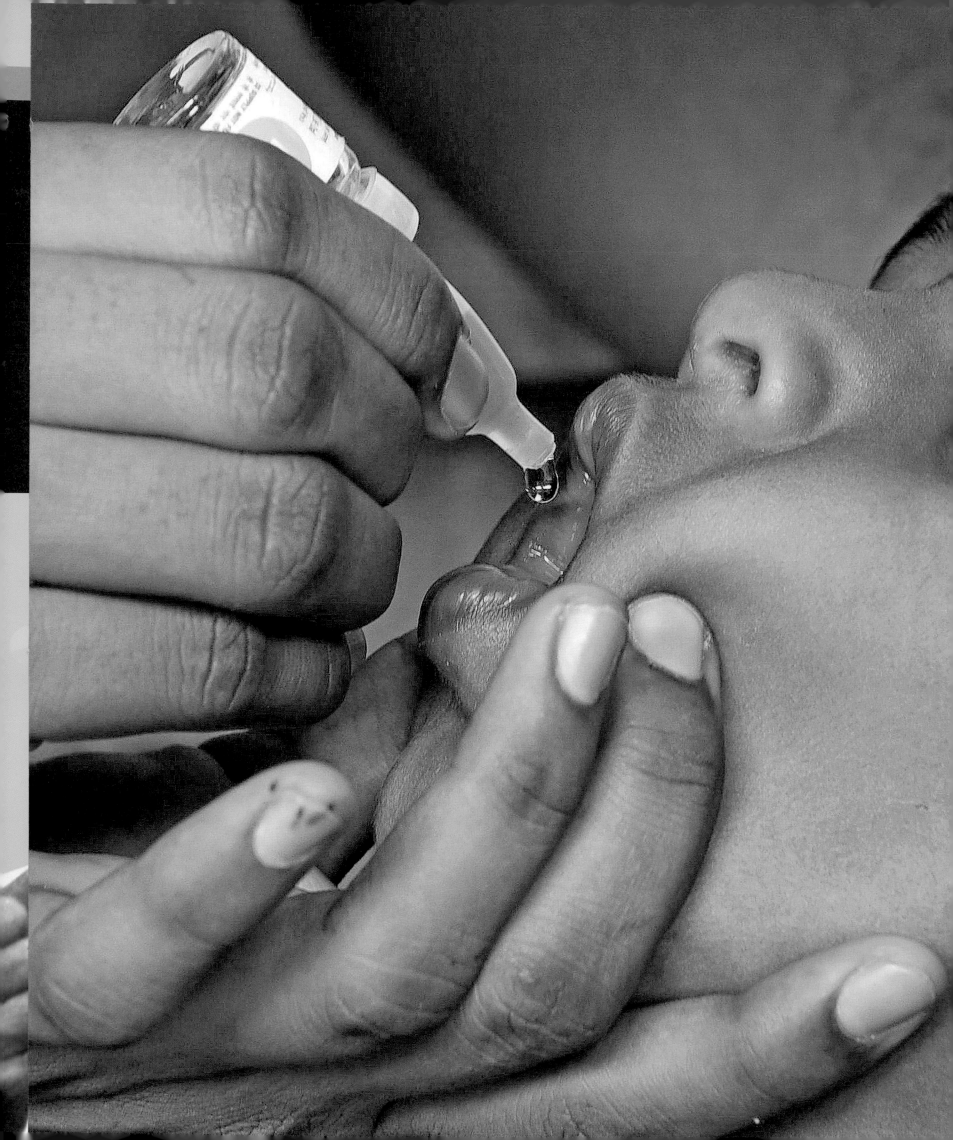

Love Is Love
On September 6, 2018, in a historic judgment, the Supreme Court of India decriminalized same-sex relationships. They ruled that the 19th-century draconian, colonial law—Section 377 of the Indian Penal Code—when applied to consenting adults, was unconstitutional. This ruling came as a great victory for the LGBTQIA+ community who have been fighting for their rights for a long time. This photograph from Kolkata, West Bengal, depicts a Pride parade, as people came together to celebrate the victory one year after the verdict.

Internet and Social Media

The digital age has changed how we communicate. Perhaps the biggest product of this age has been social media. It has emerged as an ideal tool for conversations, community building, and information dissemination. Most of all, it has become a platform for those whose voices have often been muted in society.

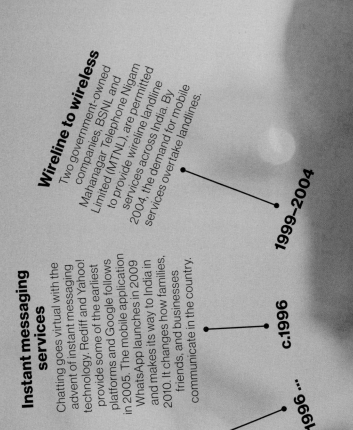

Internet in India

Connectivity has been a big factor in making social media networks accessible to India's population

- **1986** *Educational Research Network (ERNET) is launched. Its purpose is to aid academic research and is restricted to the top educational institutions of India.*

- **1995** *Videsh Sanchar Nigam Limited (VSNL) makes dial-up internet services available to everybody through modems. Though slow in speed and with technical glitches, number of subscribers go up to 10,000 in six months.*

- **2000** *Cable internet arrives. The IT Act is rolled out to deal with cyber issues.*

- **2004** *Broadband internet services, or "always-on Internet connection," is launched by BSNL (Bharat Sanchar Nigam Limited).*

- **2008–2014** *Faster connectivity is provided with the beginning of 2G, second-generation cellular services. It is followed by 3G in 2010 and 4G in 2014.*

- **2021** *Plans to launch 5G in India are currently underway.*

Wireline to wireless
1999–2004

Two government-owned companies, BSNL and Mahanagar Telephone Nigam Limited (MTNL), are permitted to provide wireline landline services across India. By 2004, the demand for mobile services overtake landlines.

Instant messaging services
c.1996

Chatting goes virtual with the advent of instant messaging technology. Rediff and Yahoo! provide some of the earliest platforms and Google follows in 2005. The mobile application WhatsApp launches in 2009 and makes its way to India in 2010. It changes how families, friends, and businesses communicate in the country.

Early online space
1996 •••

The first cybercafe opens in Mumbai with home internet access. The first cybercafe provide internet when between. These computers that a time and far and between cities are still few and across cities to computers come mushroom accessible to 'cates' making internet begins in and towns. Online banking emerges 1997. The year of hacking Indian Railway youth in first. In 1999, the Corporation that same year, the first report of online booking Catering, which enables train tickets. launches, for train tickets.

First mobile call
1995

Jyoti Basu, chief minister West Bengal makes the first call from a cell phone in Kolkata. Many years later, Kolkata becomes the first city to get the fourth generation of broadband cellular network, technology, or 4G.

BEFORE
Much before emails and text messages, communications were sent through trained animals in ancient India. During the Delhi Sultanate era, it is believed that Qutb-ud-din Aibak had a messenger post system. In 1766, Robert Clive set up the first postal service that was opened to all. The telegram service began in 1853 and ran till 2013. The telephone came to India in 1914 and the Indian Telephone Industries was formed in 1948.

Role in elections

Social media is a game changer in the 2014 general elections. Political parties use it to build their brand and develop a direct connection with their voter base. Identity politics becomes a part of their social media strategy, often via memes, hashtags, and infographics. Voters urban and rural, use the medium to become a part of larger political conversations. This trend continues in the 2019 elections.

2014

Social networking

Social networking websites emerge as connectivity improves. Orkut is an early entrant and becomes a rage among the youth as a way of staying in touch. It closes in 2014 as Facebook overtakes it in popularity. Video-sharing site YouTube, also launches with region-specific searchable content. By 2019, India becomes one of its fastest-growing audiences with almost 265 million active monthly users.

2005

Helpline for diplomacy

Twitter is abuzz when external affairs minister Sushma Swaraj helps a Pakistani mother who sends her a tweet. The request is for help with an Indian visa for her daughter's heart surgery. The external affairs ministry effectively uses the microblogging platform to directly communicate with and help people with lost passports, delayed visas, and even missing persons.

Smartphone boom

By 2015, of the 354 million internet users, 213 million internet users are mobile internet services and smartphones lead to an increase in demand. In 2017, there are 300 million smartphone users in India, with an expected 830 million users by 2022. Cheaper internet services and smartphones lead to an increase in demand. In 2017, there are 300 million smartphone users in India, with an expected 830 million users by 2022.

2015

2017

Internet population

India's internet base touches an all-time high with over 500 million active users, with cell phones being the preferred medium of internet use both in rural and urban India. India also passes the US to become the second-largest smartphone consumer in the world, after China.

2019...

Streets to tweets

Citizens take to the streets Register of Citizens. Subsequent protests become tools to inform Social media platforms use the medium to garner international support for their cause.

Indians take to the streets as Twitter and Instagram to protest the Citizenship Amendment Act and the National Register of Citizens. Social media platforms such educate and inform. Subsequent protests use the medium to build support and raise awareness, become tools to inform international support for their cause

TikTok Ban

Cross-border tensions lead to a ban on 59 Chinese apps in India due to privacy issues. This includes TikTok, a video-sharing social networking site. With more than 200 million users in India, the app has over the years become a creative outlet for millions of Indians — from rural communities to people and rural communities looking for and communities looking for their big break.

December 2019...

June 29, 2020

COVID-19 support

As the second wave of the COVID-19 pandemic sweeps through India, killing thousands, people turn to social media to communicate and for support. Volunteers use the medium to post verified information on medical supplies and hospital and oxygen availability.

2021

plebiscite
A direct vote by all members of an electorate on an important public question.

Pogrom
An organized massacre of a particular religious or ethnic group.

Prakrit
An Indo-Aryan language spoken from 500 BCE to 500 CE.

prehistory
The time before the development of civilizations and before the invention of writing.

President's rule
In India, when the rule of a state government is suspended and the central government takes charge. During President's rule, the Governor of the state becomes the constitutional head, the legislative assembly is dissolved, and elections are conducted within six months of the declaration of Emergency.

Princely states
Territories ruled by princes during the British rule in India.

privatization
A process by which an entity goes from the public to the private sector.

Puranas
Sanskrit literature describing Hindu legends, gods, and saints in an encyclopedic manner.

qawwali
Musical performance of Sufi poetry.

Raja
The title for an Indian monarch.

Rani
A queen or a *Raja's* wife.

reincarnation
Belief in rebirth of the soul that persists after bodily death.

republic
A country without a hereditary monarch or emperor. The Republic of India is governed by a Prime Minister, who is elected every five years.

reservation
Allotment of a portion of seats or jobs to a particular group that does not have the same representation or privileges as the majority of people.

riot
A violent public disturbance, usually led by a group of people against another group.

satyagraha
A Hindi term, meaning force of truth. Gandhi adopted the term to refer to a form of peaceful civil disobedience that relies upon moral force to fight against injustice.

Savarna
Communities that belong to one of the four varnas of the Hindu caste system.

Scheduled Castes
Subcommunities within the Hindu caste system who have historically faced oppression and extreme social isolation.

Scheduled Tribes
Communities who are marginalized because of their geographical isolation, and socioeconomic backwardness.

secession
Withdrawal of a region or a group of a country from the control of the central government. In India, states, such as Kashmir, and those in the northeast, have witnessed secessionist movements.

Shia
One of the two main sects in Islam. It holds Ali as the successor to the Prophet.

Sunni
One of the two main sects in Islam, traditionally following the path laid by Prophet Muhammad.

Sufism
Mysticism in Islam, guided by introspection and spiritual proximity to God.

Supreme Court
The highest judicial body in a country.

Talaq-e-biddat
A practice in Islam where three simultaneous pronouncements of the word "talaq" lead to instant divorce.

Tirthankara
A spiritual teacher in Jainism. Twenty-four *Tirthankaras* are revered as founders of Jainism.

treaty
An official, written agreement between warring parties to bring hostilities to an end.

Union territory
A federal territory in India. Unlike a state, a union territory is partly ruled by the Central government.

Upanishads
Sanskrit texts that outline the fundamental beliefs of Vedic religion.

Vedas
The oldest corpus of Sanskrit literature.

Western Ghats
A mountain range that stretches from the west coast of the Indian peninsula across Tamil Nadu, Kerala, Karnataka, Goa, and Gujarat.

Index

Page numbers in **bold** indicate main entries.